사은품

몽키와 함께하는

초등영단어 미스터

단어와 회화를 함께!!
쉽고 재미있게!!

영어 학습의 새로운 매커니즘

words
초등학생이 반드시 알아야 하는 영단어를 모았습니다.
★ '교육부 선정' 필수 단어를 예문과 함께!

subject
주제별로 단어를 모아 배우기가 쉽습니다.
★ 주제별로 단어를 모아 생활속의 활용도 높임.
★ 연관되어 있는 단어를 묶어 암기력을 최대로 발휘.

writing & speaking
쓰기와 말하기를 강화하여 기존 단어장을 뛰어넘는 영어 학습법을 제시합니다.
★ 쓰기와 말하기 Practice를 활용한 반복학습!

재미있게 공부하게 함으로써 학습동기를 높였습니다.
　★ 몽키의 설명, 그림그리기, 스티커 등 재미있는 Exercise를 통해 즐겁게 영어를 공부!

dialogue

다이얼로그 예문을 통해 자연스럽게 대화가 익숙해지므로 회화학습의 능률이 올라갑니다.
　★ 'dialogue' 예문을 통해 영어회화를 익힘.
　★ 연관되어 있는 단어를 묶어 암기력을 최대한 높임.

song

노래를 즐겁게 따라 부르면서 영어 표현에 익숙해지도록 구성되었습니다.
　★ 동요는 반복적인 리듬과 멜로디 및 가사형식을 지니고 있기 때문에 언어를 익히는 가장 좋은 방법!

원어민이 직접 녹음한 Audio를 QR코드를 통해 들으며 공부할 수 있습니다.
　★ native speaker의 소리를 듣고 정확한 발음과 강세를 익힘.

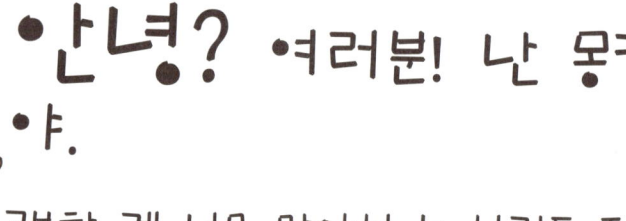

안녕? 여러분! 난 몽키야.

공부할 게 너무 많아서 놀 시간도 잠잘 시간도 부족하지?

그래서 난 우리 친구들이 너무 부담스럽지 않을 만큼만 같이 공부해 보려고 해.

이 책은 읽기와 쓰기, 듣기와 말하기를 모두 공부할 수 있도록 만들었고, 연습문제도 충분하기 때문에 워크북을 따로 사지 않아도 돼. 초등학교 필수단어를 우리 머리에 쏙쏙 들어올 만큼만 재미있게 공부할 거야.

각 과마다 먼저 새로운 단어들이 나와. 그럼 그 단어의 그림을 보고 원어민 선생님의 발음을 들으며 큰 소리로 따라 해 봐.

그런 다음 쓰기 연습을 열심히 해. 큰 소리로 읽으면서 쓰면 더 좋아. 단어와 그림을 연결시켜 보면서 다시 한 번 복습을 해.

원어민 선생님의 발음을 잘 듣고 맞는 그림을 찾기도 하고, 단어에서 빠진 알파벳을 써 넣기도 해봐. 문장을 들으면서 빈 칸에 단어를 써 넣는 것도 재미있을 거야.

그 다음엔 다양한 방법으로 지금까지 공부한 것을 연습해 볼 거야. 읽고 쓰고 들은 것을 종합해서 단어 고르기도 하고 퍼즐도 풀고 다양한 활동들을 해 봐. 간단한 대화문을 큰 소리로 따라하고 단어를 바꿔 넣으면서 연습해 봐. 말하기가 어렵지 않다는 것도 알게 될거야.

★ 각 과마다 끝에는 여러분이 재미있게 놀 수 있는 공간을 만들었어. 스티커를 붙이기도 하고, 그림도 그리고, 노래도 따라 부르면서 신나게 마무리 해보자. 나와 함께 놀다보면 어느새 영단어 실력이 쑥쑥 자라나 있을 거야.

나 몽키가 열심히 응원할게 !!

초등영단어 마스터

contents

- 알파벳과 발음기호 ... 9
- Lesson 1 family 2 ... 11
- Lesson 2 face ... 22
- song - my eyes, my nose ... 32
- Lesson 3 color ... 34
- Lesson 4 fruits & vegetables ... 47
- song - head, shoulder, knees and toes ... 59
- Lesson 5 number 1 ... 61
- Lesson 6 number 2 ... 73
- song - Ten little indian boys ... 85
- 듣기 대본 ... 87
- 정답 ... 93
- 스티커 ... 99

★ 알파벳 복습

1권에서 배웠죠? 알파벳은 대문자와 소문자가 있고, 이 알파벳이 모여 단어를 만들지요. 원어민의 발음을 듣고 따라하면서, 발음기호로는 어떻게 표시되는지도 확인해 보세요!

Aa	Bb	Cc	Dd
[eɪ]	[bi:]	[si:]	[di:]
Ee	Ff	Gg	Hh
[i:]	[ef]	[dʒi:]	[eɪtʃ]
Ii	Jj	Kk	Ll
[aɪ]	[dʒeɪ]	[keɪ]	[el]
Mm	Nn	Oo	Pp
[em]	[en]	[ou]	[pi:]
Qq	Rr	Ss	Tt
[kju:]	[ɑ:r]	[es]	[ti:]
Uu	Vv	Ww	Xx
[ju:]	[vi:]	[dʌblju:]	[eks]
Yy	Zz		
[waɪ]	[zi:]		

자음

★ 발음기호

영어의 글자가 어떻게 소리 나는지를 알려주는 기호에요.
여러 번 듣고 따라해 보세요.

	자음		
[p]	**p**ig [pɪg]	[b]	**b**ook [buk]
[t]	**t**iger [taɪgər]	[d]	**d**oor [dɔ:r]
[k]	**k**ing [kɪŋ]	[g]	**g**reen [gri:n]
[f]	**f**ood [fu:d]	[v]	fi**v**e [faɪv]
[ð]	bro**th**er [brʌðər]	[θ]	**th**ree [θri:]
[s]	**s**ea [si:]	[z]	**z**ebra [zi:brə]
[ʃ]	**sh**ark [ʃɑ:rk]	[ʒ]	plea**s**ure [pleʒər]
[tʃ]	**ch**ur**ch** [tʃə:rtʃ]	[dʒ]	**j**ean [dʒí:n]
[l]	**l**emon [lemən]	[r]	**r**ide [raɪd]
[n]	**n**ose [nouz]	[m]	**m**om [mám]
[ŋ]	ri**ng** [rɪŋ]	[j]	**y**ellow [jelou]
[h]	**h**ead [hed]	[w]	**w**orld [wə:rld]

	모음		
[a]	b**o**x [bɑ:ks]	[i]	tr**ee** [tri:]
[e]	b**e**st [best]	[u]	w**oo**d [wud]
[ɛ]	**a**ir [ɛər]	[æ]	c**a**t [kæt]
[ou]	h**o**me [houm]	[ə]	g**o**rill**a** [gərɪlə]
[ʌ]	c**u**p [kʌp]	[ɔ]	d**o**g [dɔ:g]

모음

[:] 표시는 길게 발음해야 돼!
예) [i]이 [i:]이~

Lesson 1

Family 2
가족 2

Lesson 1 Family 2

words

 다음을 듣고 큰 소리로 따라 읽어 보세요.

I   grandfather   grandmother
나   할아버지   할머니

uncle   aunt   cousin
삼촌   고모/이모   사촌

'I'는 글자체에 따라 'L'의 소문자 'l'처럼 보일 수도 있어!

Lesson 1 Family2

writing

  단어를 큰 소리로 읽으면서 써 보세요!

grandfather	grandfather
grandmother	grandmother
uncle	uncle uncle
aunt	aunt
cousin	cousin

Lesson 1 Family2

 아래 그림을 보고 알맞은 것끼리 연결해 보세요!

 할아버지	uncle
 할머니	grandfather
 삼촌	consin
 이모	grandmother
 사촌	aunt

Lesson 1 Family2

listening

 듣고 알맞은 그림에 번호를 쓰세요!

( )   ( )

( )

( )   ( )

Lesson 1 Family2

 단어를 듣고 ( ) 속에 알맞은 알파벳을 쓰세요!

1. gran( )mother

2. ( )ousin

3. g( )andfather

4. aun( )

5. u( )cle

Lesson 1 Family2

 잘 듣고 빈 칸에 알맞은 단어를 쓰세요!

1. I meet my (   )
   나는 할아버지를 만나요.

2. I meet my (   )
   나는 할머니를 만나요.

3. I meet my (   )
   나는 삼촌을 만나요.

4. I meet my (   )
   나는 이모를 만나요.

5. I meet my (   )
   나는 사촌형을 만나요.

 위의 문장을 다시 듣고 따라해 보세요!

여기서 'meet'라는 단어가 나왔지? 'meet'는 '만나다'의 뜻이야^^

Lesson 1 Family2

exercise

 가족 그림을 보고 빈 칸에 알맞은 단어를 쓰세요!

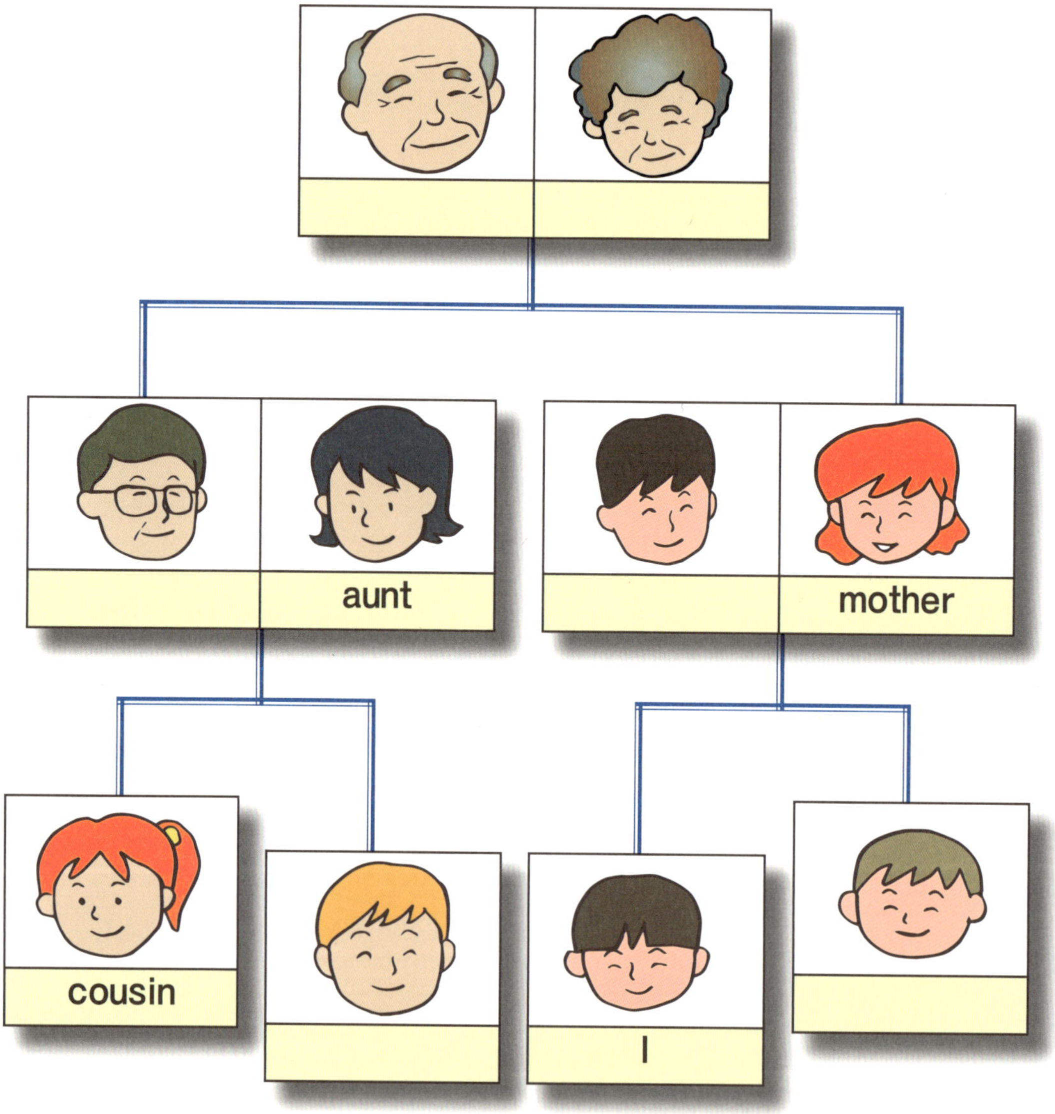

grandmother   grandfather   uncle
brother   father   cousin

Lesson 1 Family2

dialogue

 다음 대화를 듣고 큰 소리로 따라해 보세요.

이모	할아버지
A : Who is she? 그녀는 누구야? B : She is my aunt. 우리 이모야.	A : Who is he? 그 남자분은 누구야? B : He is my grandfather. 우리 할아버지야.

 그림을 보고 빈 칸에 알맞게 넣어서 말해보세요.

어머니	아버지
A : Who is she? B : She is my ( ).	A : Who is he? B : He is my ( ).

Who is 누구예요?   she 그녀   he 그
mother 어머니   father 아버지

father와 mother는 격식을 차려서 부를 때의 '아버지'와 '어머니'이고, 직접 부를 때는 보통 'dad (아빠)'와 'mom (엄마)'으로 불러^^

★ 할아버지는 무엇을 좋아하실까요? 스티커를 붙여 보세요!

스티커는 99 페이지에 있어!

★ 사촌 동생은 무엇을 좋아할까요? 스티커를 붙여 보세요!

스티커는 99 페이지에 있어!

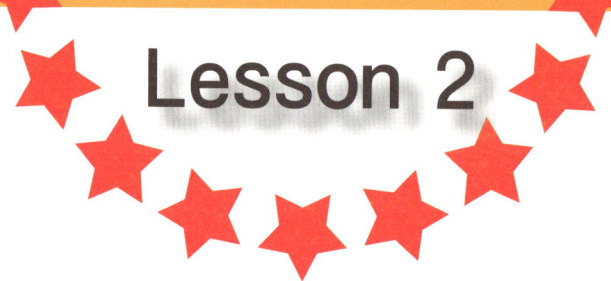

Lesson 2

Face
얼굴

Lesson 2 Face

words

 다음을 듣고 단어를 큰 소리로 따라해 보세요.

face(얼굴)

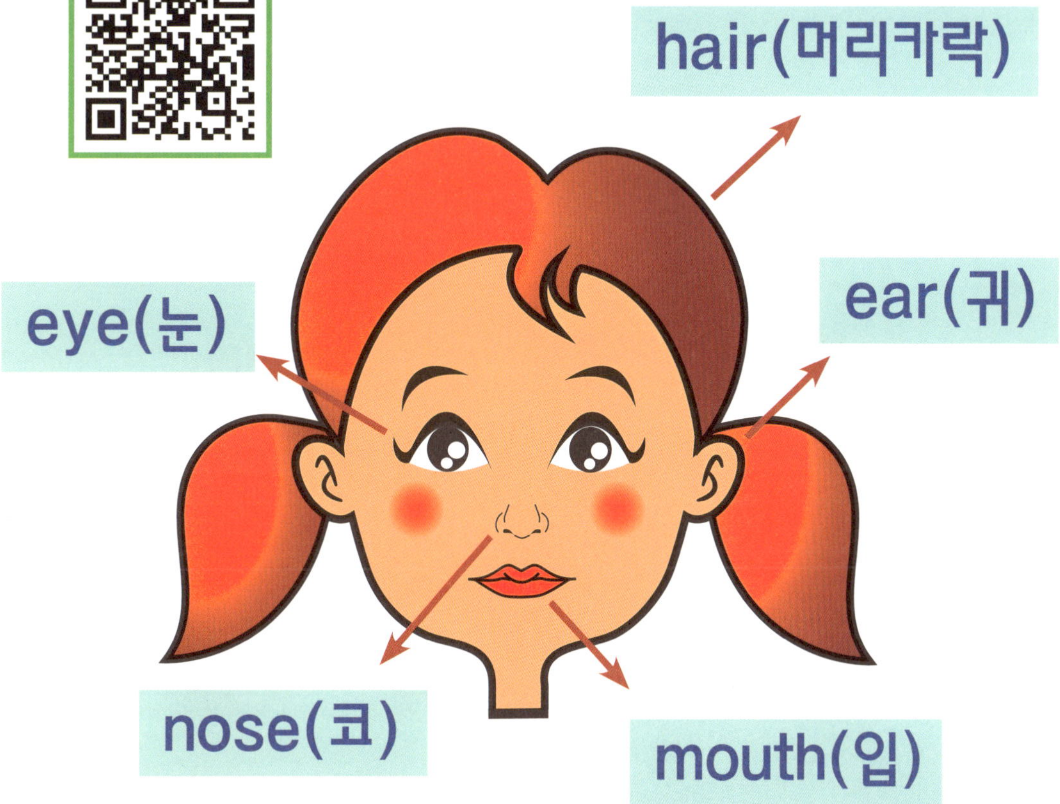

- hair(머리카락)
- eye(눈)
- ear(귀)
- nose(코)
- mouth(입)

Lesson 2 Face

writing

  단어를 큰 소리로 읽으면서 써 보세요!

face	**face** face face face face face face face
hair	**hair** hair hair hair hair hair hair hair
eye	**eye** eye eye eye eye eye eye eye
nose	**nose** nose nose nose nose nose nose nose
mouth	**mouth** mouth mouth mouth mouth mouth
ear	**ear** ear ear ear ear ear ear ear

Lesson 2 Face

 아래 그림을 보고 알맞은 것끼리 연결해 보세요!

ear image	nose
girl face	ear
nose	face
eye	mouth
hair	hair
mouth	eye

Lesson 2 Face

listening

 듣고 알맞은 그림에 번호를 쓰세요!

( )   ( )

( )   ( )

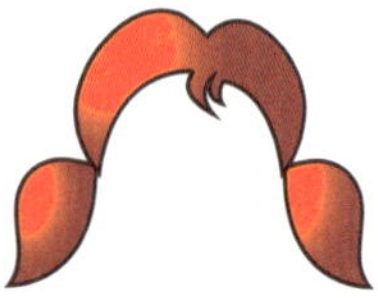

( )   ( )

Lesson 2 Face

 단어를 듣고 ( ) 속에 알맞은 알파벳을 써 넣으세요!

1. f( )ce

2. ha( )r

3. ( )ye

4. no( )e

5. ea( )

6. mo( )th

Lesson 2 Face

 잘 듣고 빈 칸에 알맞은 단어를 쓰세요!

1. This is my (   )
   이건 내 얼굴이에요.
2. This is my (   )
   이건 내 눈이에요.
3. This is my (   )
   이건 내 코에요.
4. This is my (   )
   이건 내 입이에요.
5. This is my (   )
   이건 내 귀에요.
6. This is my (   )
   이건 내 머리카락이에요.

 위의 문장을 다시 듣고 따라해 보세요!

'this is'라는 문장이 나왔지?
'this is'는 '이건 ~예요'의 뜻이야^^
그리고 'I'가 아니더라도 문장의 첫 글자는
대문자로 써야 한다는 것도 기억해!

Lesson 2 Face

exercise

 배운 단어를 찾아 하나로 묶고, 아래에 쓰세요!

n	m	c	e	k
b	o	d	y	b
i	u	s	e	y
f	t	o	e	i
o	h	a	i	r

eye

Lesson 2 Face

dialogue

 다음을 듣고 단어를 큰 소리로 따라해 보세요.

	A : Do you like your face? 네 얼굴이 마음에 들어? B : Yes, I like my face. 응, 난 내 얼굴이 좋아.
	A : Do you like your nose? 네 코가 마음에 들어? B : Yes, I like my nose. 응, 난 내 코가 좋아.

 보기에 주어진 단어를 이용하여 연습해 보세요.

	A : Do you like your (　　　　)? B : Yes, I like my (　　　　).
	mouth　　eye　　ear　　hair

'Do you like~?' : ~를 좋아해요?'
또는 '~가 마음에 들어요?'
'I like ~ : 나는 ~를 좋아해요' 의 뜻이야 ^^

Lesson 2 Face

★ 꼬마 도깨비 친구의 얼굴에 눈, 코, 입을 그려 주세요!

Let's sing a song

♬ QR코드로 노래를 듣고 따라 불러보세요!

My eyes, my nose

My eyes, my nose,
my mouth, my ears.

My eyes, my nose,
my mouth, my ears.

My eyes, my nose,
my mouth, my ears.

We all clap hands together.

♪ My eyes, my nose를 다시 들으면서 빈 칸에 알맞은 알파벳을 넣어보세요!

My eyes, my nose

My ( )yes, my nose,
my mouth, my ears.

My eyes, my ( )ose,
my mou( )h, my ears.

My eyes, my nose,
my mouth, my e( )rs.

We all clap hands
together.

Lesson 3

Color
색깔

Lesson 3 Color

words

 다음을 듣고 단어를 큰 소리로 따라해 보세요.

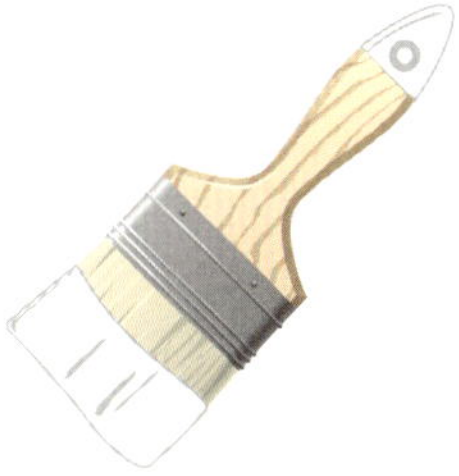 white 하얀색	 yellow 노란색	 red 빨간색
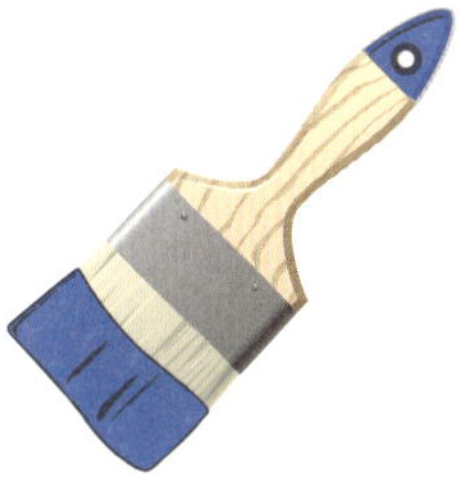 blue 파란색	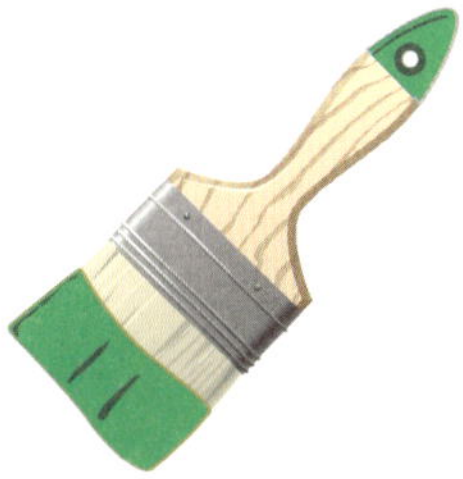 green 초록색	 black 검정색
 pink 분홍색	 gray 회색	 brown 갈색

Lesson 3 Color

writing

  단어를 큰 소리로 읽으면서 써 보세요!

color	**color** color color
	color color color
white	**white** white white
	white white white
yellow	**yellow** yellow yellow
	yellow yellow yellow
red	**red** red red red
	red red red red
blue	**blue** blue blue blue
	blue blue blue blue

Lesson 3 Color

green	**green** green green
	green green green
black	**black** black black
	black black black
pink	**pink** pink pink pink
	pink pink pink pink
gray	**gray** gray gray gray
	gray gray gray gray
brown	**brown** brown brown
	brown brown brown

Lesson 3 Color

 아래 그림을 보고 알맞은 것끼리 연결해 보세요!

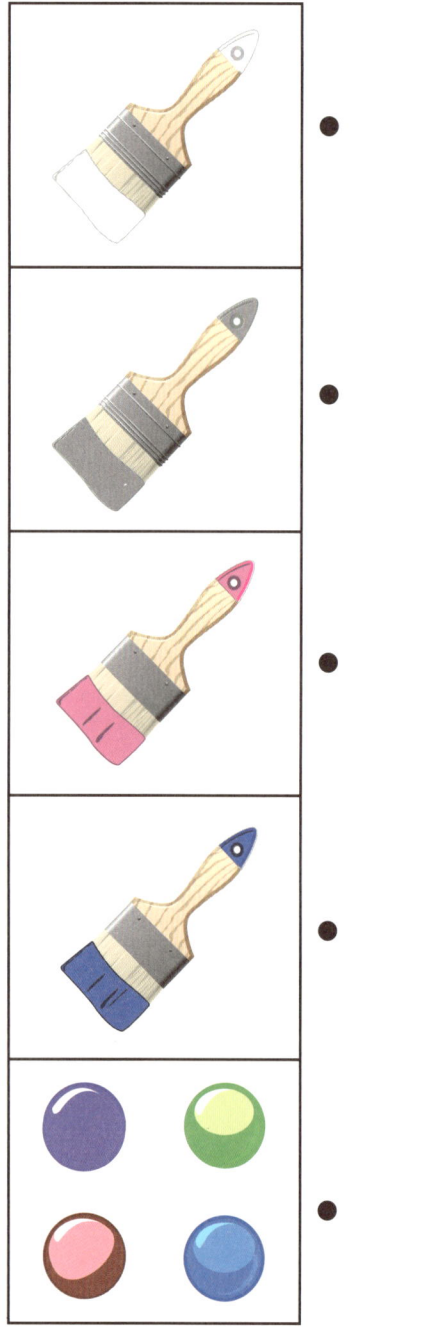

Lesson 3 Color

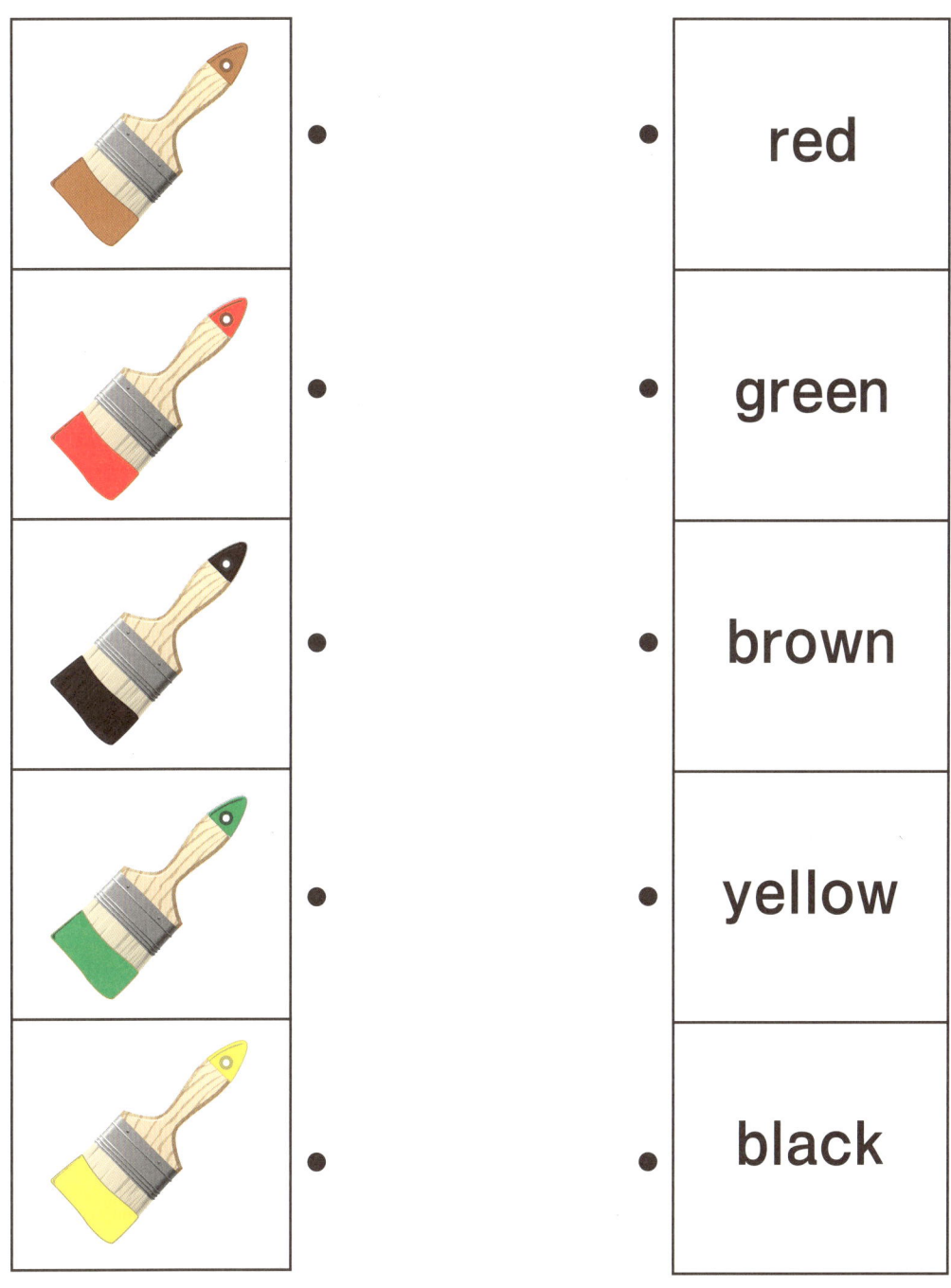

Lesson 3 Color

listening

 듣고 알맞은 그림에 번호를 쓰세요!

( )   ( )   ( )

( )   ( )   ( )

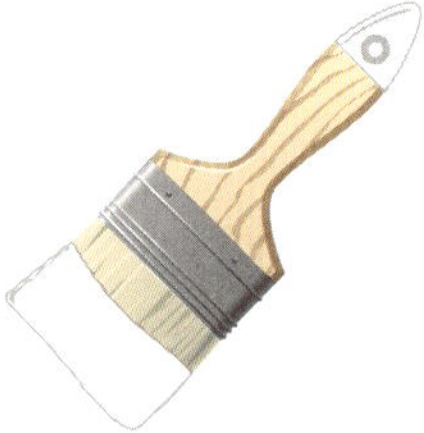

( )   ( )   ( )

Lesson 3 Color

 단어를 듣고 ( ) 속에 알맞은 알파벳을 써 넣으세요!

1. (　)ed　　2. yello(　)　　3. pi(　)k

4. g(　)een　　5. bl(　)ck　　6. (　)ray

7. wh(　)te　　8. blu(　)　　9. bro(　)n

Lesson 3 Color

exercise

 잘 듣고 빈 칸에 알맞은 단어를 쓰세요!

1. This banana is (   )
   이 바나나는 노란색이에요.

2. This ball is (   )
   이 공은 초록색이에요.

3. This hat is (   )
   이 모자는 빨간색이에요.

4. This balloon is (   )
   이 풍선은 파란색이에요.

5. These shoes are (   )
   이 구두는 검정색이에요.

여기서 'these'와 'are'라는 단어가 나왔지? 'these'는 'this'의 복수형(둘 이상)이고, 'are'는 복수형의 '~이다'의 뜻이야 단수형(하나)은 'is'야^^

Lesson 3 Color

6. This ribbon is (   )
   이 리본은 분홍색이에요.

7. My puppy is (   )
   내 강아지는 하얀색이에요.

8. That elephant is (   )
   저 코끼리는 회색이에요.

9. That bear is (   )
   저 곰은 갈색이에요.

10. My favorite (   ) is green.
    내가 가장 좋아하는 색은 초록색이에요.

👄 위의 문장을 여러 번 듣고 따라해 보세요!

this 이   that 저   banana 바나나   ball 공
hat 모자   balloon 풍선   shoes 구두   ribbon 리본
puppy 강아지   elephant 코끼리   bear 곰

Lesson 3 Color

dialogue

 다음 대화를 듣고 큰 소리로 따라해 보세요.

A : What is your favorite color? 네가 제일 좋아하는 색은 뭐야? B : I like yellow. 난 노란색을 좋아해.	A : Is your puppy white? 네 강아지는 흰색이야? B : No, he is white and brown. 아니, 흰색하고 갈색이야.

 보기에 주어진 단어를 이용하여 연습해 보세요.

A : What is your favorite color?
B : I like (   )

| white | black | green | pink | blue | gray |
| yellow | red | brown | | | |

What is 뭐예요?   your 너의
favorite 가장 좋아하는

★ 비온 뒤 하늘에 무지개가 떴어요. 예쁘게 색칠하세요!

재미있는 상식 이야기

각 나라별 다른 소리

■ 강아지 짖는 소리
▷ 한국 : 멍멍
▷ 일본 : 왕왕
▷ 중국 : 왕
▷ 영국 : 바우 바우
▷ 독일 : 바우 바우
▷ 프랑스 : 우아 우아
▷ 스페인 : 구아우 구아우

■ 종 치는 소리
▷ 한국 : 땡땡
▷ 일본 : 공공
▷ 중국 : 딩당당
▷ 프랑스 : 당동 당동
▷ 영국 미국 : 딩동 딩동

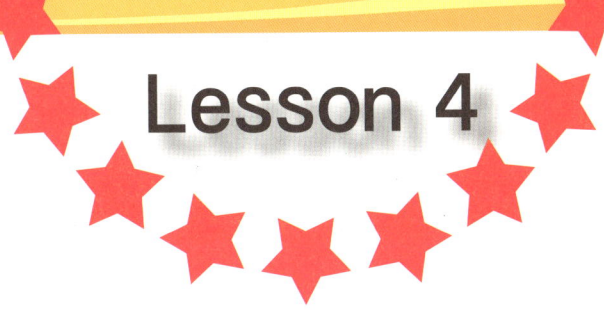

Lesson 4

Fruits & Vegetables
과일과 채소

Lesson 4 Fruits & Vegetables

words

 다음을 듣고 단어를 큰 소리로 따라해 보세요.

fruits 과일	**apple** 사과	**banana** 바나나
orange 오렌지	**grape** 포도	**pear** 배
vegetables 채소	**potato** 감자	**onion** 양파
carrot 당근	**tomato** 토마토	**corn** 옥수수

Lesson 4 Fruits & Vegetables

writing

  단어를 큰 소리로 읽으면서 써 보세요!

fruits	fruits fruits fruits
	fruits fruits fruits
apple	apple apple apple
	apple apple apple
banana	banana banana banana
	banana banana banana
grape	grape grape grape
	grape grape grape
orange	orange orange orange
	orange orange orange
pear	pear pear pear
	pear pear pear

Lesson 4 Fruits & Vegetables

vegetables	vegetables vegetables vegetables vegetables
potato	potato potato potato potato potato
onion	onion onion onion onion onion
carrot	carrot carrot carrot carrot carrot
tomato	tomato tomato tomato tomato tomato
corn	corn corn corn corn corn

채소에는 우리 몸에 필요한
영양분이 아주 많이 들어 있대~
그러니까 친구들도 많이 먹어야 해^^

Lesson 4 Fruits & Vegetables

 아래 그림을 보고 알맞은 것끼리 연결해 보세요!

- apple
- fruits
- banana
- grape
- pear
- orange

Lesson 4 Fruits & Vegetables

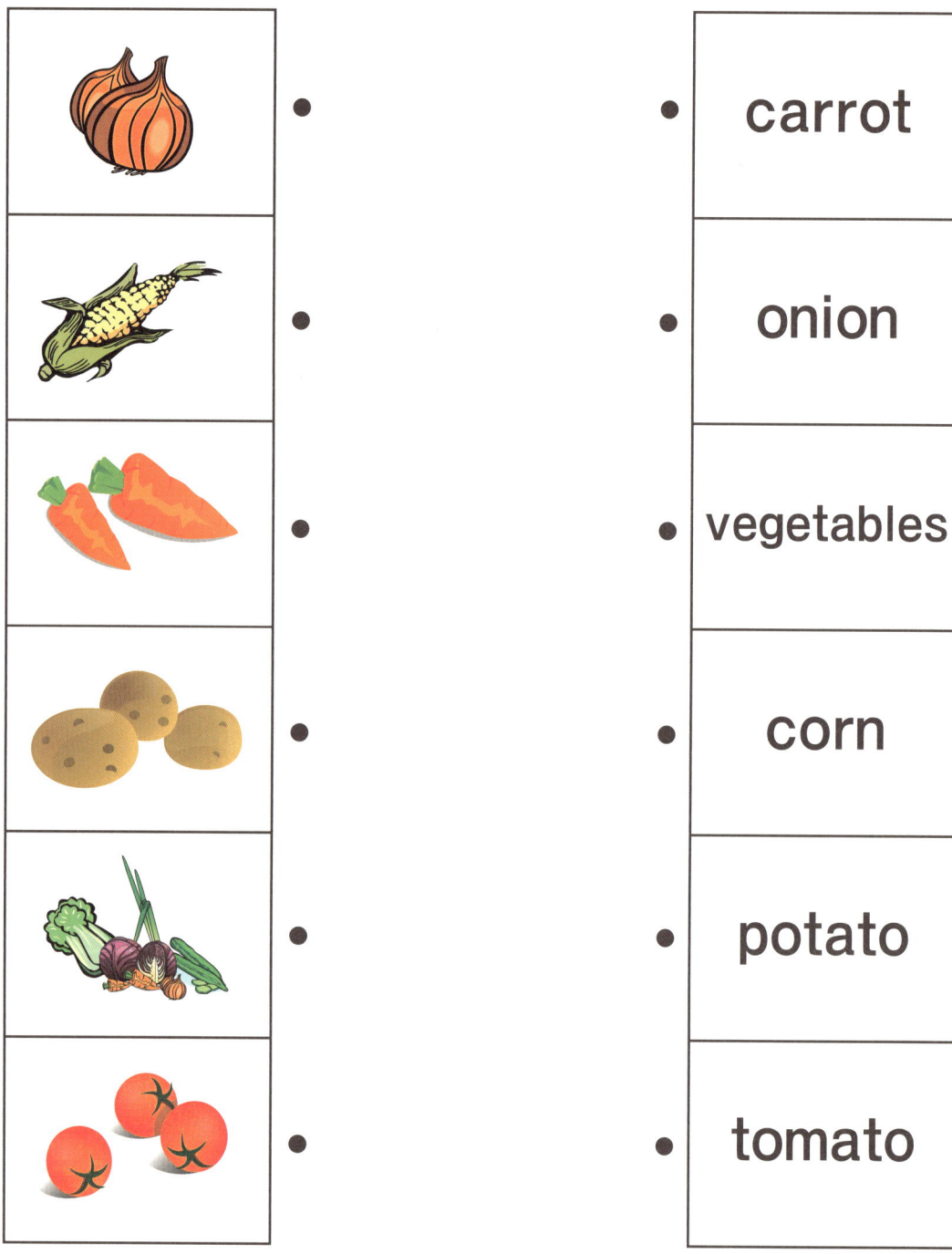

Lesson 4 Fruits & Vegetables

listening

 듣고 알맞은 그림에 번호를 쓰세요!

( )   ( )   ( )

( )   ( )   ( )

( )   ( )   ( )

Lesson 4 Fruits & Vegetables

 단어를 듣고 (　) 속에 알맞은 알파벳을 써 넣으세요!

1. app(　)e　　2. po(　)ato　　3. (　)nion

4. carr(　)t　　5. g(　)ape　　6. to(　)ato

7. (　)ear　　8. orang(　)　　9. (　)ruits

Lesson 4 Fruits & Vegetables

exercise

 문장을 듣고 빈 칸에 알맞은 단어를 쓰세요!

1. I like (　　　　　)

   나는 포도를 좋아해요.

2. There is an (　　　　　)

   (거기) 사과 한 개가 있어요.

3. This (　　　　　) is white.

   이 양파는 하얀색이에요.

4. There are two (　　　　es)

   토마토가 두 개 있어요.

5. The rabbit likes (　　　　　)

   토끼는 당근을 좋아해요.

　　👄 위의 문장을 여러 번 듣고 따라해 보세요!

There is (거기)에 있다
There are '(거기)에 있다' 복수형
The 그

Lesson 4 Fruits & Vegetables

 다음 중 fruit에 해당하는 것을 골라 동그라미(O) 하세요!

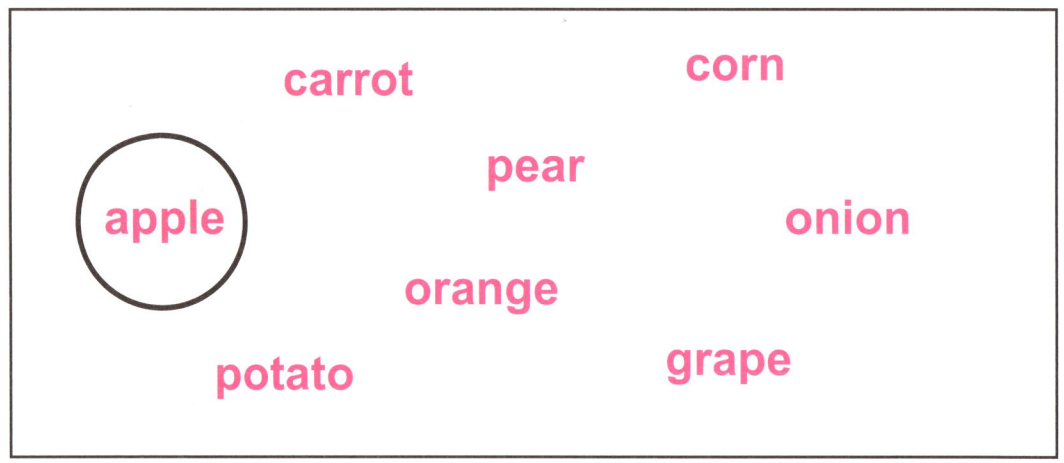

 그림에 알맞은 단어를 골라 동그라미 하세요!

1		two (onions / tomatoes) one (potato / tomato)
2		two (onions / carrots) one (tomato / orange)

Lesson 4 Fruits & Vegetables

dialogue

 다음 대화를 듣고 큰 소리로 따라해 보세요.

A : What is your favorite fruit? 네가 제일 좋아하는 과일이 뭐야? B : I like oranges. 난 오렌지를 좋아해.	A : What is in the box? 상자 안에 뭐가 있어? B : It's a carrot. 당근이야.

 보기에 주어진 단어를 이용하여 연습해 보세요.

A : What is your favorite fruit?
B : I like (   )

banana   grape   apple   orange   pear

'in' '안에', 'box'는 '상자'야
'in the box' '상자 안에'라는 뜻이 되지

★ 엄마가 시장에 다녀오셨어요. 과일과 채소를 구분하여 큰 접시에 담아 보세요! (스티커 붙이기)

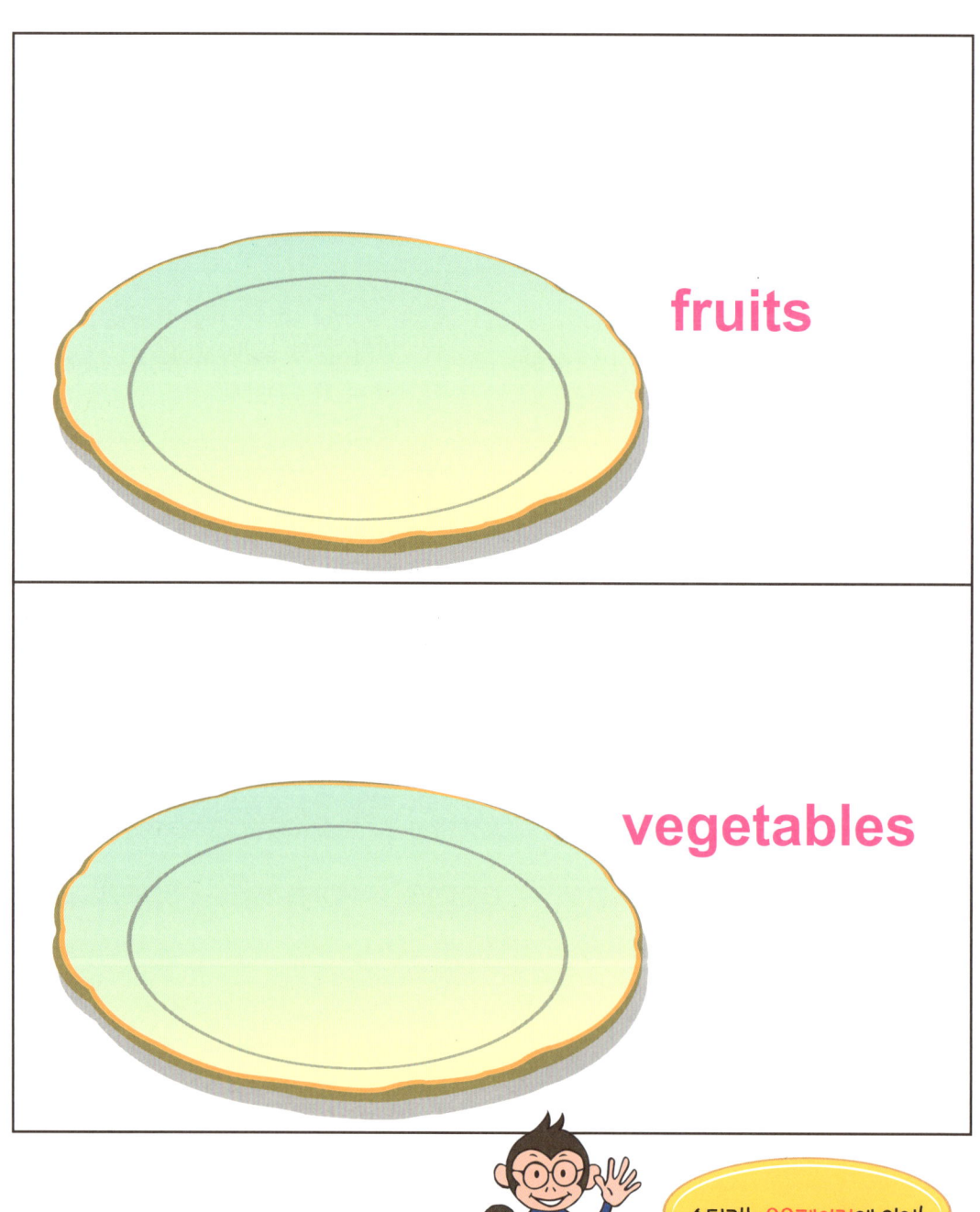

♫ QR코드로 노래를 듣고 따라 불러보세요!

Head, shoulder, knees and toes

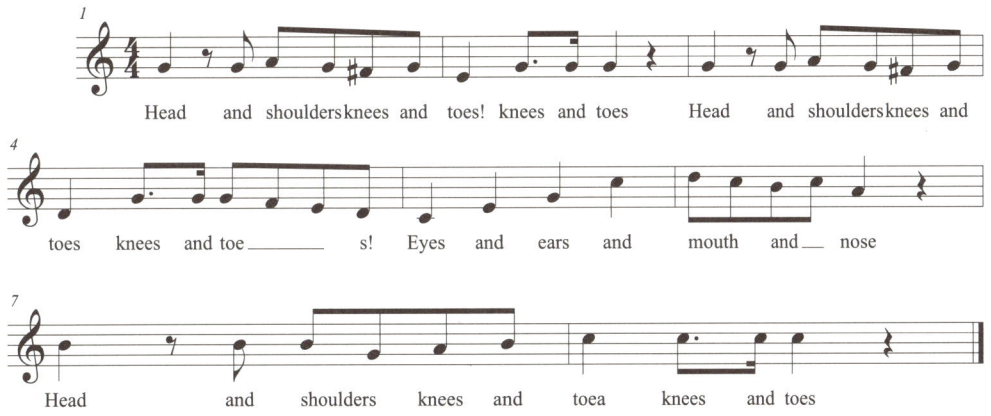

🎵 율동과 함께 'Head, shoulder, knees and toes' 를 다시 불러 보세요!

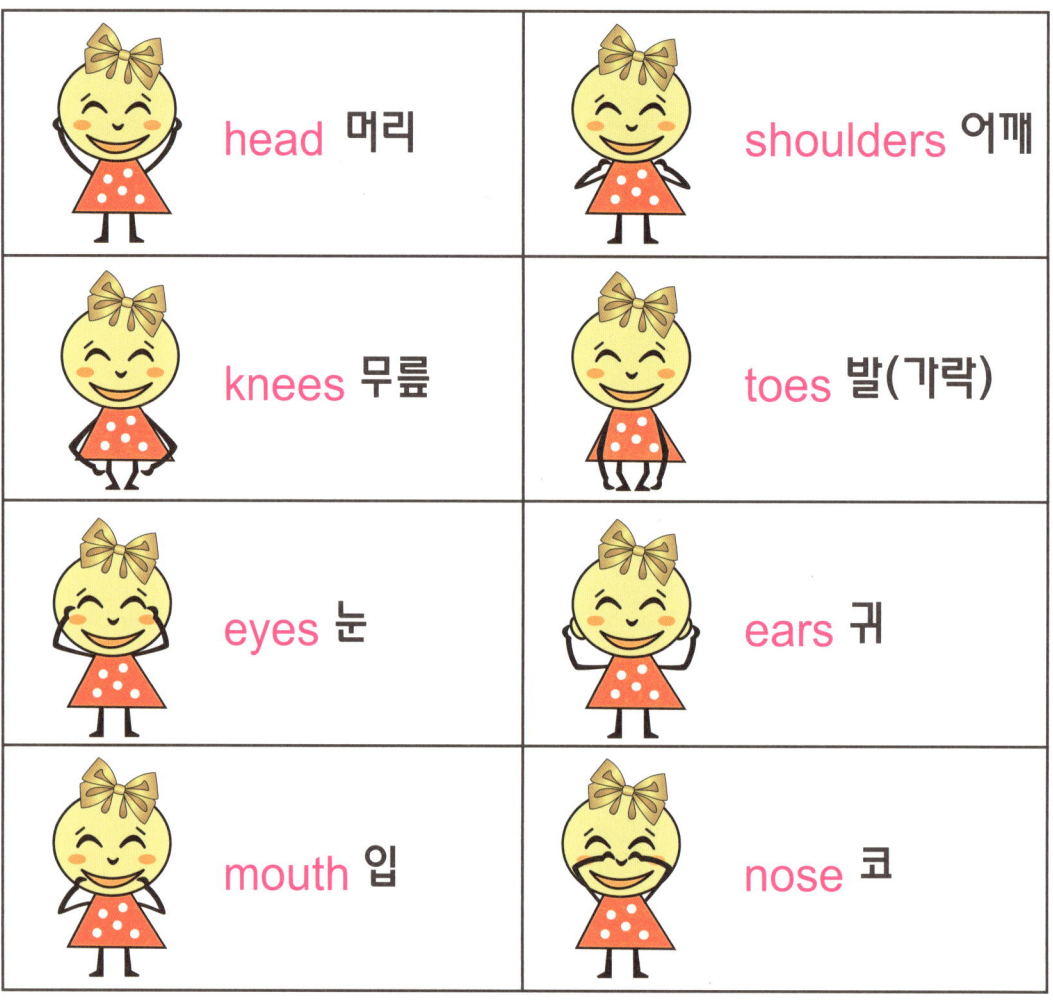

Head shoulders knees and toes
Knees and toes
Head shoulders knees and toes
Knees and toes
eyes and ears and mouth and nose
Head shoulders knees and toes
Knees and toes

Lesson 5

Number 1
숫자

Lesson 5 Number 1

words

 다음을 듣고 단어를 큰 소리로 따라 읽어 보세요.

	number	0	zero
1	one	2	two
3	three	4	four
5	five	6	six
7	seven	8	eight
9	nine	10	ten

Lesson 5 Number 1

writing

  단어를 큰 소리로 읽으면서 써 보세요!

number	number number number
	number number number
zero	zero zero zero
	zero zero zero zero
one	one one one
	one one one one
two	two two two
	two two two two
three	three three
	three three three
four	four four four
	four four four four

Lesson 5 Number 1

5 five	five five five five five five five five
6 six	six six six six six six six six
7 seven	seven seven seven seven seven seven
8 eight	eight eight eight eight eight eight
9 nine	nine nine nine nine nine nine nine nine
10 ten	ten ten ten ten ten ten ten ten

Lesson 5 Number 1

 아래 그림을 보고 알맞은 것끼리 연결해 보세요!

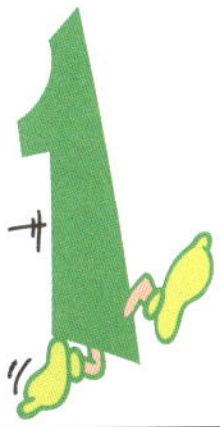

1 •	• nine
3 •	• one
8 •	• three
9 •	• zero
0 •	• five
5 •	• eight

Lesson 5 Number 1

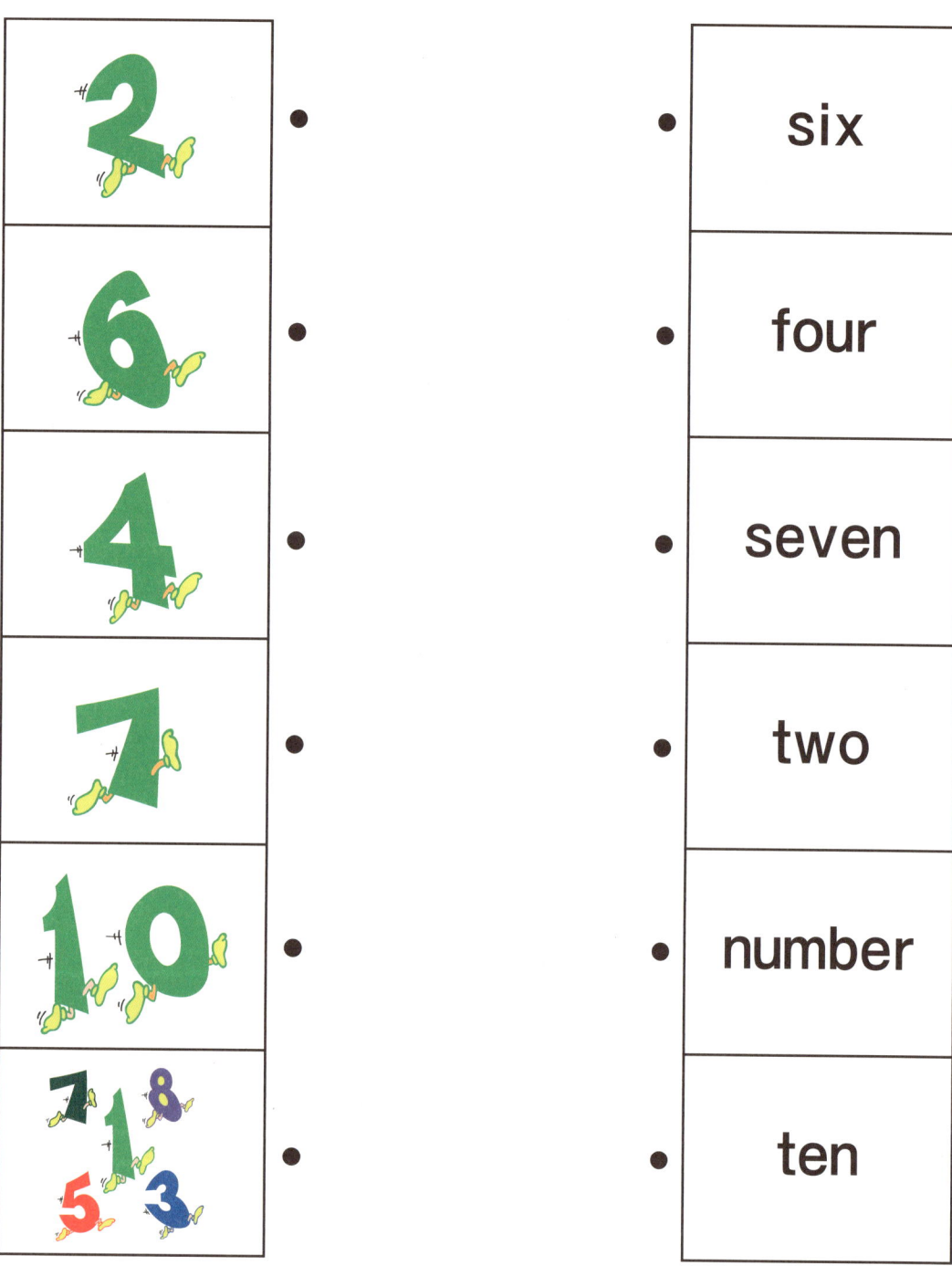

Lesson 5 Number 1

listening

 듣고 알맞은 그림에 번호를 쓰세요!

바람개비	( )	우산	( )
구슬 10개	( )	하트	( )
토마토	( )	자동차	( )
음표	( )	음료수	( )
눈사람	( )	책	( )

Lesson 5 Number 1

 단어를 듣고 ( ) 속에 알맞은 알파벳을 써 넣으세요!

1. t( )o   2. ( )our   3. ei( )ht

4. se( )en   5. si( )   6. ( )ne

7. f( )ve   8. t( )ree   9. ( )ero

10. n( )mber   11. ni( )e   12. te( )

Lesson 5 Number 1

exercise

 그림에 알맞은 숫자를 골라 O표 하세요!

1		one	two	five
2		six	seven	four
3		nine	ten	eight
4		nine	six	zero
5		five	two	four
6		ten	one	three

Lesson 5 Number 1

dialogue

 다음 대화를 듣고 큰 소리로 따라해 보세요.

A : How old are you? 　　너는 몇 살이야? B : I'm nine years old. 　　나는 아홉 살이야.	A : How old is she? 　　그녀는 몇 살이야? B : She is five years old. 　　그녀는 다섯 살이야.

 그림을 보고 빈 칸에 알맞게 넣어서 말해보세요.

A : How old are you?

B : I am (　　　　) years old.

A : How old is she?

B : She is (　　　　) years old.

| one | two | three | four | five |
| six | seven | eight | nine | ten |

'How old~'는 '몇 살이냐?'고 물을 때 사용하는 것이고,
'~years old'는 '(몇) 살이다'라고 대답할 때
쓰는 거야^^

Lesson 5 Number 1

★ 내 방 안에 여러 가지 물건이 있지요. 세어보고 숫자를 영어로 써보세요!

재미있는 상식 이야기

미키 마우스는 미국 월트 디즈니 회사의 상징적인 캐릭터야. 세계에서 제일 유명할 걸. 그런데 이 미키마우스가 벌써 80살이 훨씬 넘었다는 거 알아?

미키마우스가 세상에 처음 나온 건 1928년 11월 28일 '증기선 윌리'라는 작품에서였대. 성격이 지금보다 훨씬 급하고 폭력적인 캐릭터였는데, 부모님들이 그 만화영화를 보고 항의를 해서 지금의 성격을 가진 미키 마우스가 되었대.

아마 그 급한 성격은 친구인 도널드 덕이 가져갔나봐. 이름도 원래는 '모티머 마우스'라고 했었는데, 월트 디즈니의 부인인 릴리안 디즈니가 '미키 마우스'라고 이름을 붙였다지?

이봐 친구들… 나도 80이 넘었다구~

Lesson 6

Number 2
숫자 2

Lesson 6 Number 2

words

 다음을 듣고 단어를 큰 소리로 따라해 보세요.

11	eleven	**12**	twelve
13	thirteen	**14**	fourteen
15	fifteen	**16**	sixteen
17	seventeen	**18**	eighteen
19	nineteen	**20**	twenty

Lesson 6 Number 2

10	ten	**20**	twenty
30	thirty	**40**	forty
50	fifty	**60**	sixty
70	seventy	**80**	eighty
90	ninety	**100**	one hundred

한 세기는 100년이야...
'one hundred years'가 한 세기 라는 말이지... 세기를 영어로 'century' 라고 하는 것도 알아두자구^^

Lesson 6 Number 2

writing

  단어를 큰 소리로 읽으면서 써 보세요!

11 eleven	**eleven** eleven eleven eleven eleven eleven
12 twelve	**twelve** twelve twelve twelve twelve twelve
13 thirteen	**thirteen** thirteen thirteen thirteen thirteen thirteen
14 fourteen	**fourteen** fourteen fourteen fourteen fourteen fourteen
15 fifteen	**fifteen** fifteen fifteen fifteen fifteen fifteen
16 sixteen	**sixteen** sixteen sixteen sixteen sixteen sixteen

Lesson 6 Number 2

17 seventeen	seventeen	seventeen seventeen
	seventeen	seventeen seventeen
18 eighteen	eighteen	eighteen eighteen
	eighteen	eighteen eighteen
19 nineteen	nineteen	nineteen nineteen
	nineteen	nineteen nineteen
20 twenty	twenty	twenty twenty
	twenty	twenty twenty
30 thirty	thirty	thirty thirty
	thirty	thirty thirty
100 one hundred	hundred	hundred hundred
	hundred	hundred hundred

혹시 '틴에이저'라는 말 들어봤니? 영어로 'teenager'는 '청소년'을 뜻하는데 숫자 13~19까지 뒤에 'teen'이 들어가서 생겨난 말이라구^^

Lesson 6 Number 2

 아래 그림을 보고 알맞은 것끼리 연결해 보세요!

12	fifteen
14	twelve
15	thirteen
13	fourteen
17	eleven
11	seventeen

Lesson 6 Number 2

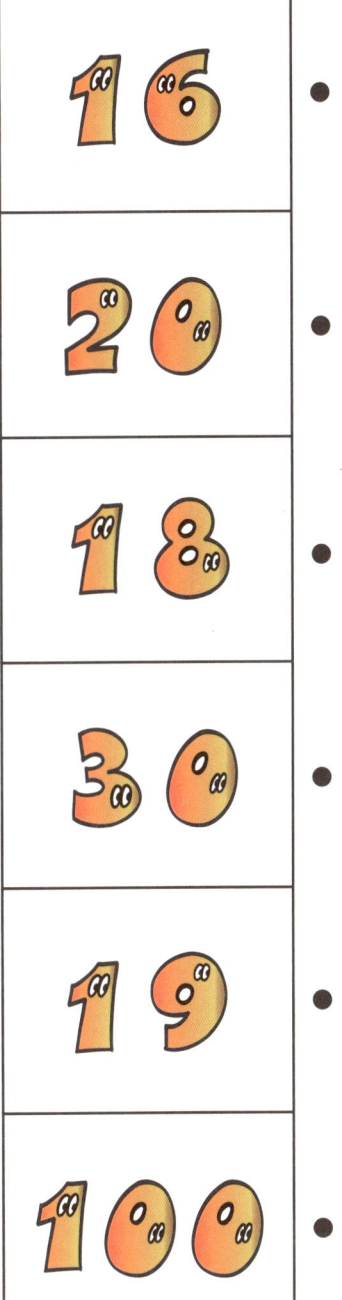

- 16
- 20
- 18
- 30
- 19
- 100

- eighteen
- twenty
- sixteen
- thirty
- one hundred
- nineteen

Lesson 6 Number 2

listening

 다시 듣고 숫자를 영어로 써 보세요!

11 (   )   12 (   )

13 (   )   14 (   )

15 (   )   16 (   )

17 (   )   18 (   )

19 (   )   20 (   )

30 (   )   100 (   )

Lesson 6 Number 2

 단어를 듣고 (　) 속에 알맞은 알파벳을 써 넣으세요!

1. fo(　)rteen	2. ele(　)en
3. t(　)enty	4. sevent(　)en
5. fi(　)teen	6. twe(　)ve
7. t(　)irteen	8. si(　)teen
9. (　)ighteen	10. thirt(　)
11. one (　)undred	12. nine(　)een

Lesson 6 Number 2

exercise

✏️ 다음 숫자를 나타내는 단어에 ✓ 표시 하세요!

1 **20** twenty ☐
        twelve ☐

2 **12** twelve ☐
        twenty ☐

3 **15** fifteen ☐
        fourteen ☐

4 **17** sixteen ☐
        seventeen ☐

5 **30** thirteen ☐
        thirty ☐

6 **100** one hundred ☐
        two hundred ☐

Lesson 6 Number 2

dialogue

 다음 대화를 듣고 큰 소리로 따라해 보세요.

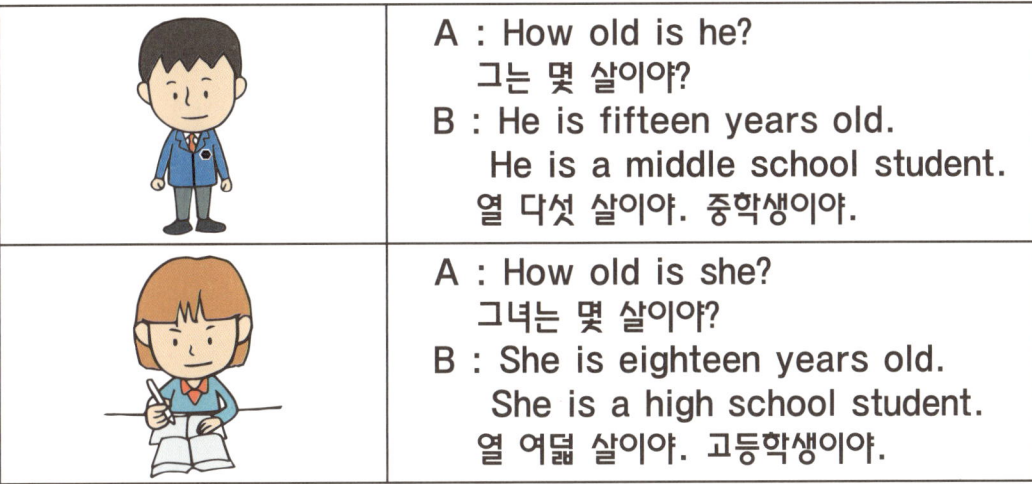

	A : How old is he? 그는 몇 살이야? B : He is fifteen years old. He is a middle school student. 열 다섯 살이야. 중학생이야.
	A : How old is she? 그녀는 몇 살이야? B : She is eighteen years old. She is a high school student. 열 여덟 살이야. 고등학생이야.

 예문을 보고 빈 칸에 알맞게 넣어서 말해보세요.

A : How old are you?

B : I am (   ) years old.

A : How old is she?

B : She is (   ) years old.

---

eleven   twelve   thirteen   fourteen   fifteen

sixteen   seventeen   eighteen   nineteen

elementary school 초등학교
middle school 중학교
high school 고등학교
student 학생

★ 형제, 자매, 사촌, 친구들의 얼굴을 그려보고 나이를 숫자와 영어로 써보세요!

♫ QR코드로 노래를 듣고 따라 불러보세요!

Ten little indian boys

one little two little three little in-di ans Four little Five little Six little in-di ans

Seven little Eight little Nine little in-di ans Ten little in-di ans boy

🎵 음악에 맞춰 인디언처럼 춤추면서 노래를 다시 불러봅시다!

One little, two little, three little Indians

Four little, five little, six little Indians

Seven little, eight little, nine little Indians

Ten little Indian boys.

Ten little, nine little, eight little Indians

Seven little, six little, five little Indians

Four little, three little, two little Indians

One little Indian boy.

듣기대본

P 9

a b c d e f g h i j k l m n o p q r s t u v w x y z

P 10

자음			
[p]	**p**ig [pɪg]	[b]	**b**ook [buk]
[t]	**t**iger [taɪgər]	[d]	**d**oor [dɔ:r]
[k]	**k**ing [kɪŋ]	[g]	**g**reen [gri:n]
[f]	**f**ood [fu:d]	[v]	fi**v**e [faɪv]
[ð]	bro**th**er [brʌðər]	[θ]	**th**ree [θri:]
[s]	**s**ea [si:]	[z]	**z**ebra [zi:brə]
[ʃ]	**sh**ark [ʃɑ:rk]	[ʒ]	plea**s**ure [pleʒər]
[tʃ]	**ch**urch [tʃə:rtʃ]	[dʒ]	**j**ean [dʒí:n]
[l]	**l**emon [lemən]	[r]	**r**ide [raɪd]
[n]	**n**ose [nouz]	[m]	**m**om [mám]
[ŋ]	ri**ng** [rɪŋ]	[j]	**y**ellow [jelou]
[h]	**h**ead [hed]	[w]	**w**orld [wə:rld]

모음			
[a]	b**o**x [bɑ:ks]	[i]	tr**ee** [tri:]
[e]	b**e**st [best]	[u]	w**oo**d [wud]
[ɛ]	**ai**r [ɛər]	[æ]	c**a**t [kæt]
[ou]	h**o**me [houm]	[ə]	g**o**rilla [gərɪlə]
[ʌ]	c**u**p [kʌp]	[ɔ]	d**o**g [dɔ:g]

1과

P 12

I grandfather grandmother   uncle   aunt   cousin

P 15

1) grandfather   2) cousin   3) grandmother
4) aunt   5) uncle

P 16

1) grandmother   2) cousin   3) grandfather
4) aunt   5) uncle

듣기대본

P 17
1. I meet my grandfather
2. I meet my grandmother
3. I meet my uncle
4. I meet my aunt
5. I meet my cousin

P 19
A : Who is she?
B : She is my aunt.

A : Who is he?
B : He is my grandfather.

2과
P 23
face   hair   eye   nose   mouth   ear

P 26
1) nose 2)hair 3)face 4)mouth 5)ear 6)eye
P 27
1) face 2)hair 3)eye 4)nose 5)ear 6)mouth

P 28
1. This is my face
2. This is my eye
3. This is mynose
4. This is my mouth
5. This is my ear
6. This is my hair

P 30
A : Do you like your face ?
B : Yes, I like my face.

A : Do you like your nose?
B : Yes, I like my nose.

P 32
song - My eyes, my nose

3과
P 35

white	yellow	red
blue	green	black
pink	gray	brown

P 40
1) white 2) green 3) brown 4) yellow 5) pink
6) red 7) black 8) blue 9) gray

P 41
1) red 2) yellow 3) pink 4) green 5) black
6) gray 7) white 8) blue 9) brown

P 42~43
1. This banana is yellow.
2. This ball is green.
3. This hat is red.
4. This balloon is blue.
5. These shoes are black.
6. This ribbon is pink.
7. My puppy is white.
8. That elephant is gray.
9. That bear is brown.
10. My favorite color is green.

P 42
A : What is your favorite color?
B : I like yellow.
A : Is your puppy white?
B : No, he is white and brown.

듣기대본

4과

P 48 words

fruits	apple	banana
orange	grape	pear
vegetables	potato	onion
carrot	tomato	corn

P 53

1) apple 2) grape 3) onion 4) potato
5) orange 6) corn 7) carrot 8) tomato 9) pear

P 54

1) apple 2) potato 3) onion 4) carrot 5) grape
6) tomato 7) pear 8) orange 9) fruits

P 55

1. I like grape.
2. There is an apple.
3. This onion is white.
4. There are two tomatoes.
5. The rabbit likes carrot.

P 57

A : What is your favorite fruit?
B : I like oranges.

A : What is in the box ?
B : It's a carrot.

P 59

sing -Head, shoulder, knees and toes

5과

P 62

number	zero
one	two
three	four
five	six
seven	eight
nine	ten

P 67

1) two   2) seven   3) four   4) eight   5) nine
6) five   7) three   8) six   9) one   10) ten

P 68

1) two   2) four   3) eight   4) seven   5) six
6) one   7) five   8) three   9) zero   10) ten
11) nine   12) number

P 70

A : How old are you?
B : I'm nine years old.

A : How old is she?
B : She is five years old.

6과

P 74

eleven	twelve
thirteen	fourteen
fifteen	sixteen
seventeen	eighteen
nineteen	twenty

듣기대본

P 75

ten	twenty
thirty	forty
fifty	sixty
seventy	eighty
ninety	one hundred

P 80

1) eleven 2) twelve 3) thirteen 4) fourteen 5) fifteen
6) sixteen 7) seventeen 8) eighteen 9) nineteen 10) twenty
11) thirty 12) one hundred

P 81

1) fourteen   2)eleven   3)twenty 4)seventeen
5) fifteen   6)twelve   7)thirteen 8)sixteen
9)eighteen   10)thirty   11)one hundred   12)nineteen

P 83

A : How old is he?
B : He is fifteen years old.
   He is a middle school student.

A : How old is she?
B : She is eighteen years old.
   She is a high school student.

P 85

sing - Ten little indian boys

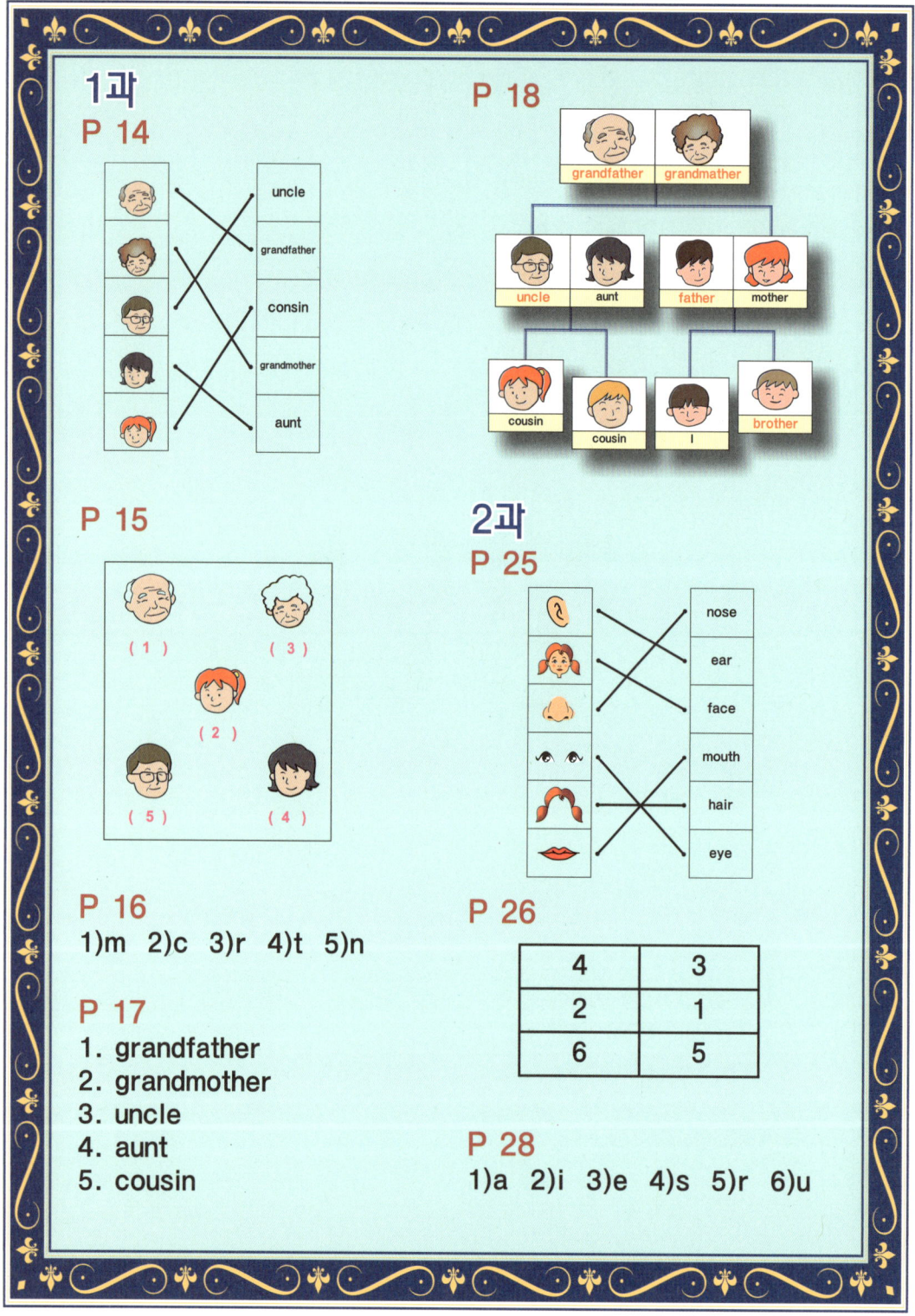

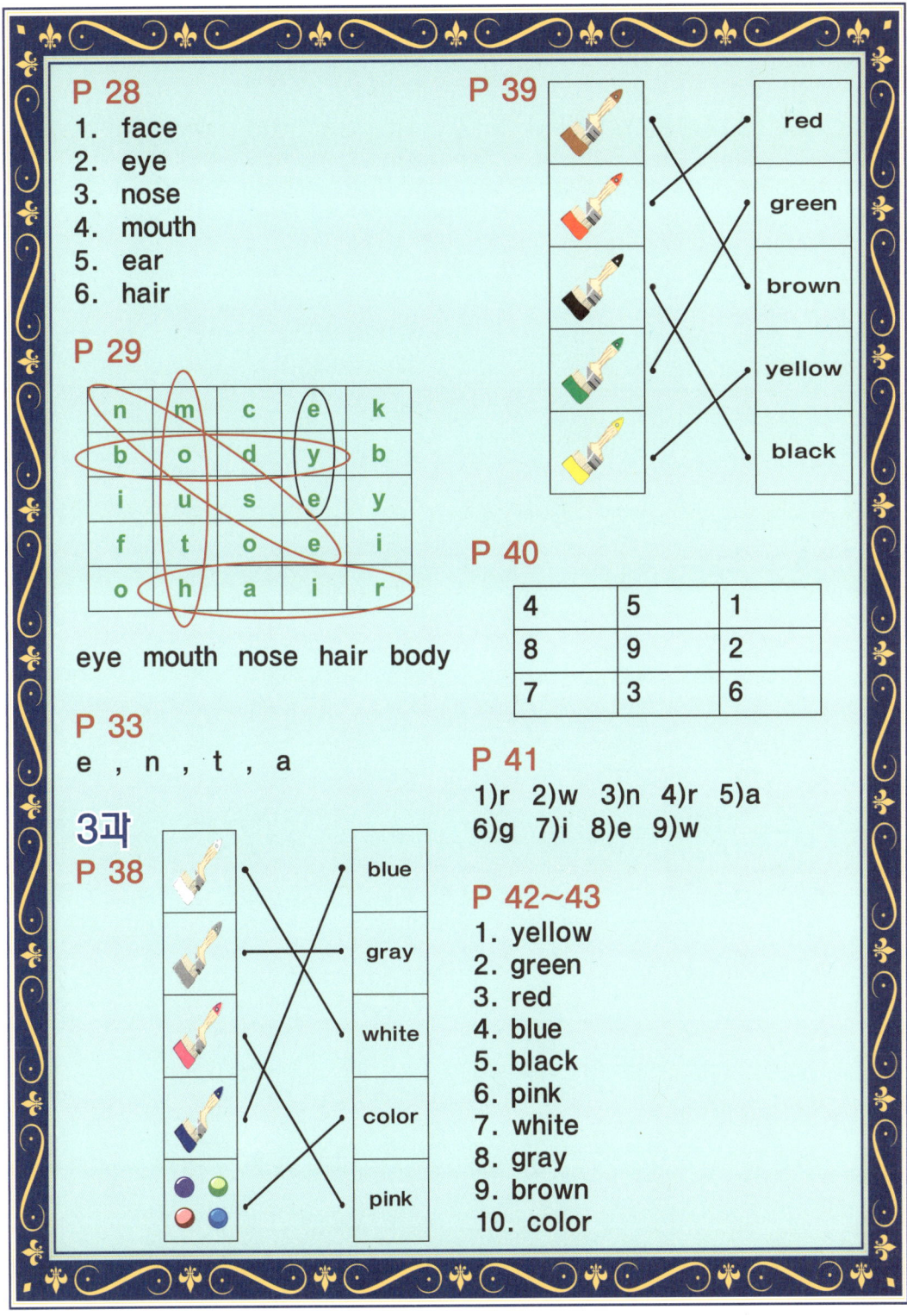

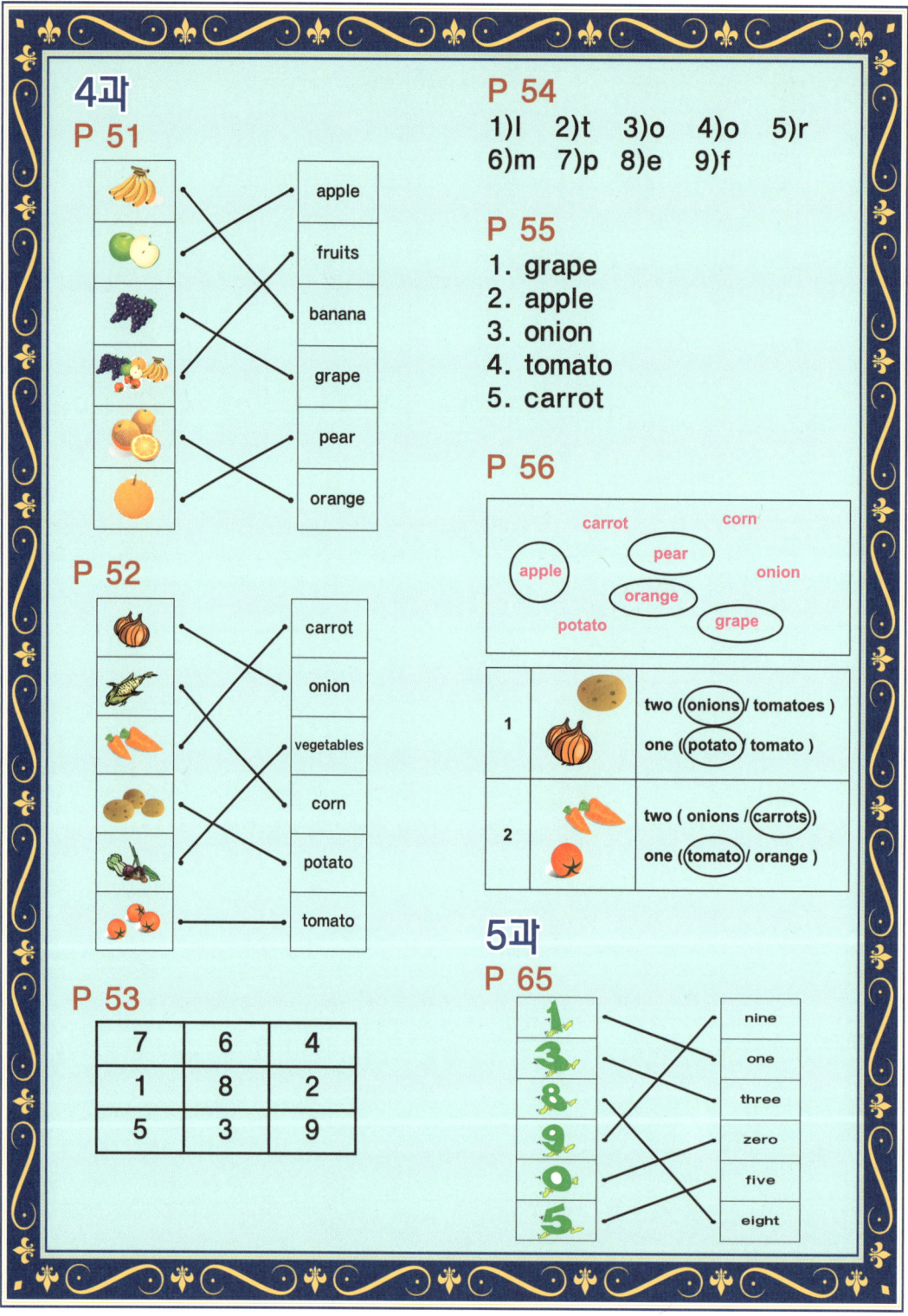

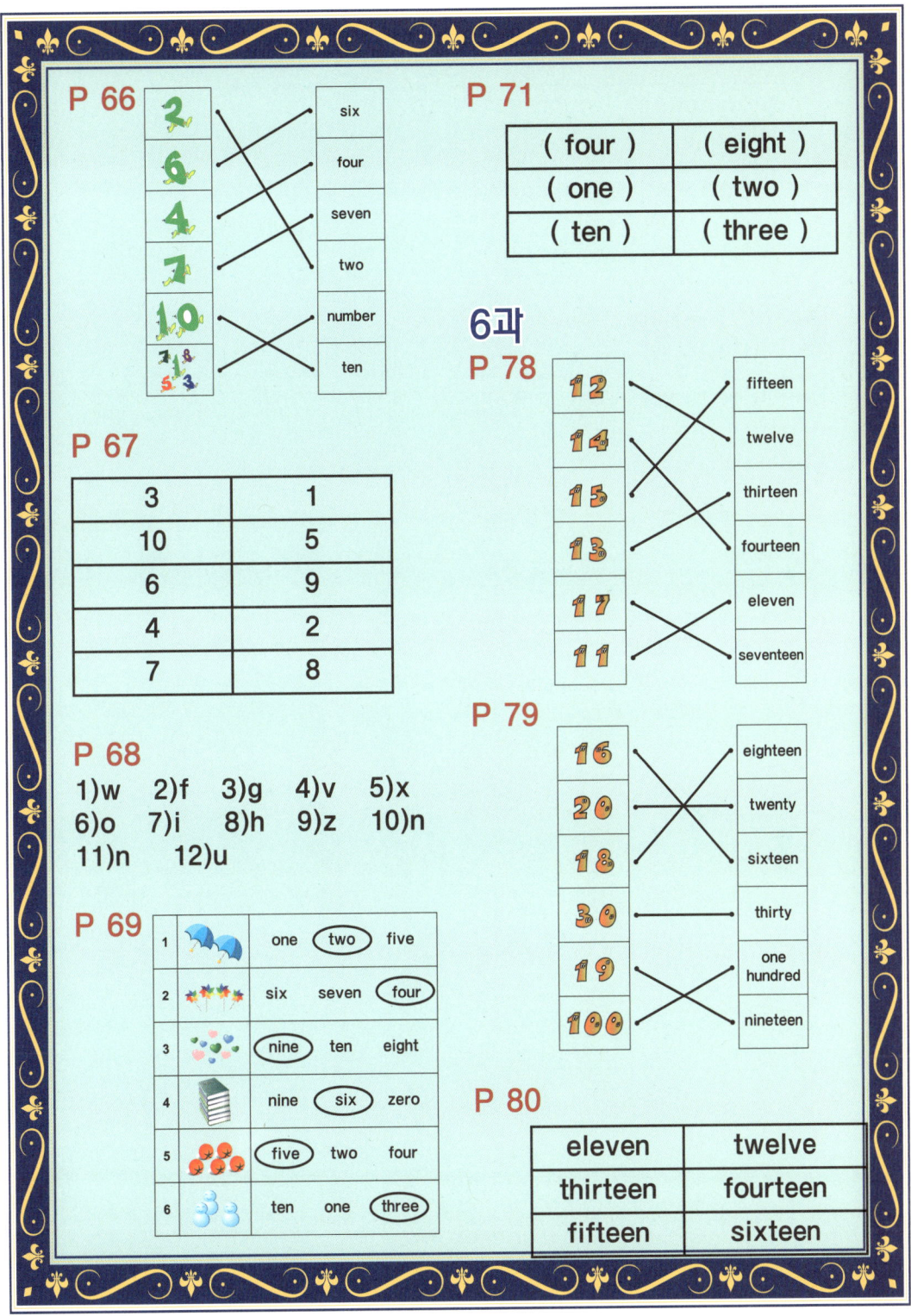

정답

seventeen	eighteen
nineteen	twenty
thirty	one hundred

P 81

1)u   2)v   3)w   4)e
5)f   6)l   7)h   8)x
9)e   10)y   11)h   12)t

P 82

1. 20 — twenty ✓ / twelve ☐
2. 12 — twelve ✓ / twenty ☐
3. 15 — fifteen ✓ / fourteen ☐
4. 17 — sixteen ☐ / seventeen ✓
5. 30 — thirteen ☐ / thirty ✓
6. 100 — one hundred ✓ / two hundred ☐

스티커

P 20, 21

P 58